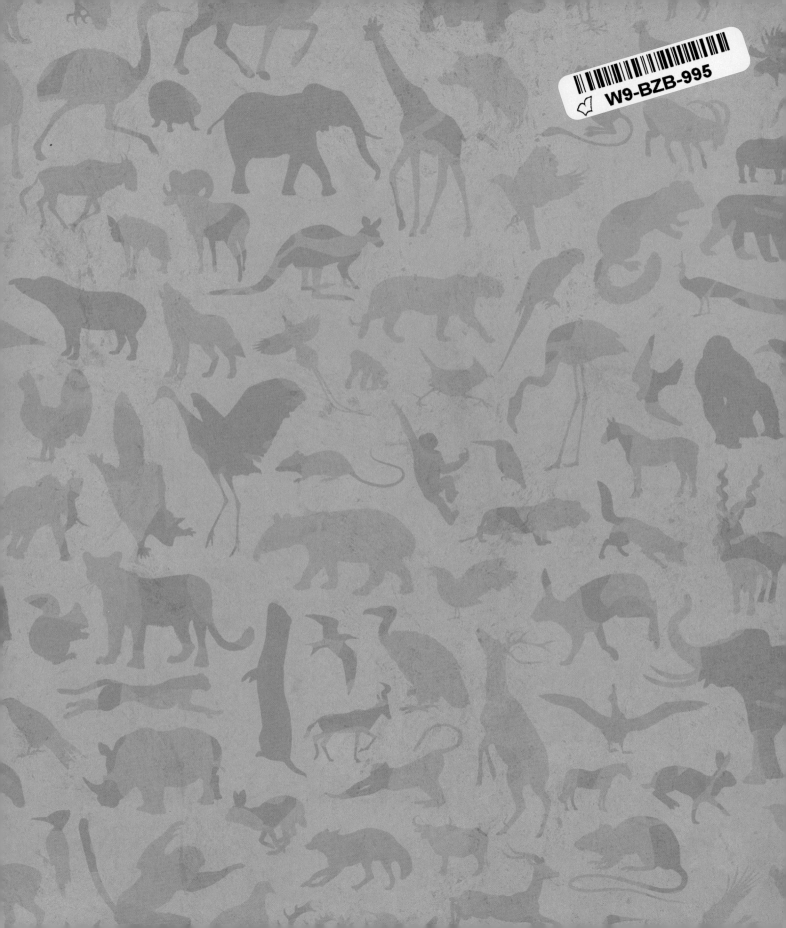

Weird and Wonderful

Show-offs

KINGFISHER
LONDON & NEW YORK

Published in the United States by Kingfisher,
175 Fifth Ave., New York, NY 10010

Kingfisher is an imprint of Macmillan
Children's Books, London.
All rights reserved.

Distributed in the U.S. by Macmillan,
175 Fifth Ave., New York, NY 10010

Library of Congress Cataloging-in-Publication
data has been applied for.

Kingfisher books are available for special
promotions and premiums. For details contact:
Special Markets Department, Macmillan,
175 Fifth Ave., New York, NY 10010.

For more information, please visit
www.kingfisherbooks.com

Conceived and produced by
Weldon Owen Pty Ltd
59–61 Victoria Street, McMahons Point
Sydney NSW 2060, Australia
weldonowenpublishing.com

Copyright © 2011 Weldon Owen Pty Ltd

WELDON OWEN PTY LTD
Managing Director Kay Scarlett
Publisher Corinne Roberts
Creative Director Sue Burk
**Senior Vice President,
International Sales** Stuart Laurence
Sales Manager, North America Ellen Towell
**Administration Manager,
International Sales** Kristine Ravn

Managing Editor Helen Bateman
Consultant Professor Phil Whitfield
Design Concept Cooling Brown Ltd
Designer Gabrielle Green
Images Manager Trucie Henderson
Production Director Todd Rechner
Production and Prepress Controller Mike Crowton

ISBN: 978-0-7534-6722-0

Printed and bound in China by 1010 Printing Int Ltd.

The paper used in the manufacture of this book is
sourced from wood grown in sustainable forests.
It complies with the Environmental Management
System Standard ISO 14001:2004

A WELDON OWEN PRODUCTION

animalplanet.com
animalplanetbooks.com

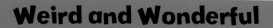

Weird and Wonderful
Show-offs

Margaret McPhee

Astonishing Animals

Bizarre Behavior

KINGFISHER

NEW YORK

Contents

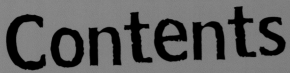

6 COLORFUL CREATURES

8 Bright and beautiful

10 Warning colors

12 Black and white

14 Spotlight on butterflies

16 Making light

18 Changing colors

20 See-through

22 Dressed to impress

24 LAND, AIR, AND SEA

26 Scare tactics

28 Making a noise

30 Spotlight on hummingbirds

32 Aerial acrobatics

34 Everyday living

36 Spikes and shells

38 **COURTSHIP AND MATING**

40 Finding a mate

(42) **Spotlight** on sounds and signals

44 Birdsong

46 Undersea communication

48 Fighting for a mate

(50) **Spotlight** on giant beetles

52 Showy feathers

54 Elaborate dances

56 Courtship rituals

(58) **Spotlight** on bowerbirds

60 Gift giving

62 Glossary

64 Index

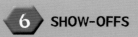

COLORFUL CREATURES

Animals use colors in many ways. Vivid color can be a signal to attract a mate or a device to threaten a rival. Certain colors are warnings to would-be predators to stay away. Against a colorful background, bold colors and patterns can even help an animal hide.

Brightly colored clown fish swim safely in sea anemones.

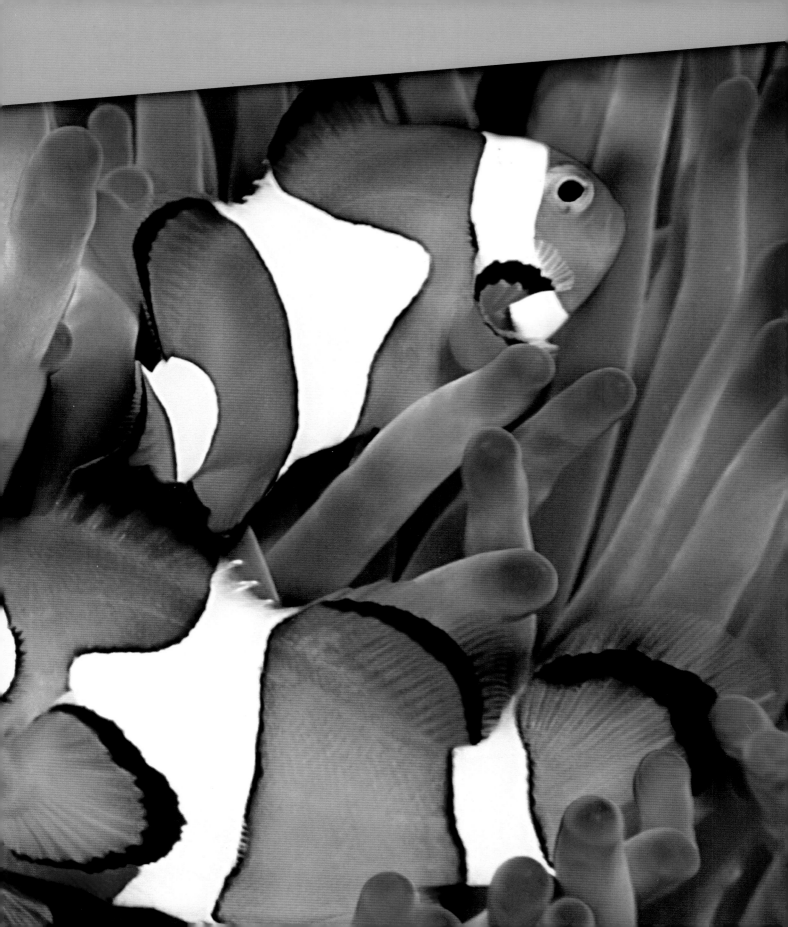

Bright and beautiful

Animals come in an extraordinary number of patterns and colors—reds, yellows, greens, and blues, as well as white, black, and grays. Some of the most vibrantly colored live in the tropical rainforests where birds dress in rainbow hues, butterflies flash brightly in the sun, and jewel-like beetles dazzle in steamy forests.

In the pink Vast flocks of flamingos feed in the shallow lakes of eastern Africa. The birds get their color from pink pigment extracted from the shrimp and algae they eat.

Blue in the face The head and neck of the cassowary have no feathers, and its bare skin is brightly colored. The colors develop when the birds are about one year old.

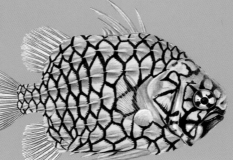

Australian pineapple fish

The mouth of a pineapple fish has a green glow.

This changes to red as the fish gets older.

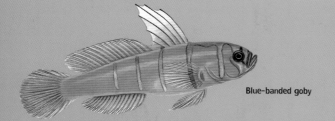

Blue-banded goby

Technicolor world Vibrant colors help tropical fish blend into the bright backgrounds of the warm, clear waters. Dramatic markings break up the outline of the body and confuse predators.

Steel blue killifish

Flying colors With a wingspan of more than 3 feet (1 m), these large and powerful red-and-green macaws soar above the forest canopy, their long tails trailing like bright streamers.

Flashy fur Gaudily colored snub-nosed monkeys live in the forests of central China. Fiery red-gold fur covers the shoulders and frames the pale blue face of the female.

Don't touch! The bright colors and bold markings are a signal to predators that this swallowtail caterpillar has a foul taste and should be left alone. The toxins come from its diet of poisonous plants.

Warning colors

The red, yellow, and black colors of some animals, especially in bold patterns or stripes, act as an alarm signal. They flash the message to would-be predators that these creatures are poisonous, stinging, or foul-tasting. Some harmless creatures copy these colors to trick predators into avoiding them as well.

Look out! Both the conspicuous stripes of the adult Colorado beetle (left) and the black spots of its larvae warn predators that these insects will not make pleasant eating.

Deadly South American poison-arrow frogs take toxins from the ants and spiders on which they feed. Rainforest peoples coat blowgun darts with poison from the frogs to kill prey.

The skin of the blue poison-arrow frog contains enough toxins to kill a human being.

Poison-arrow frogs gleam like jewels in the leafy rainforest.

Toxins are released through tiny pores in the frog's skin.

The **skin** of some poison-arrow frogs can produce a powerful painkilling medicine.

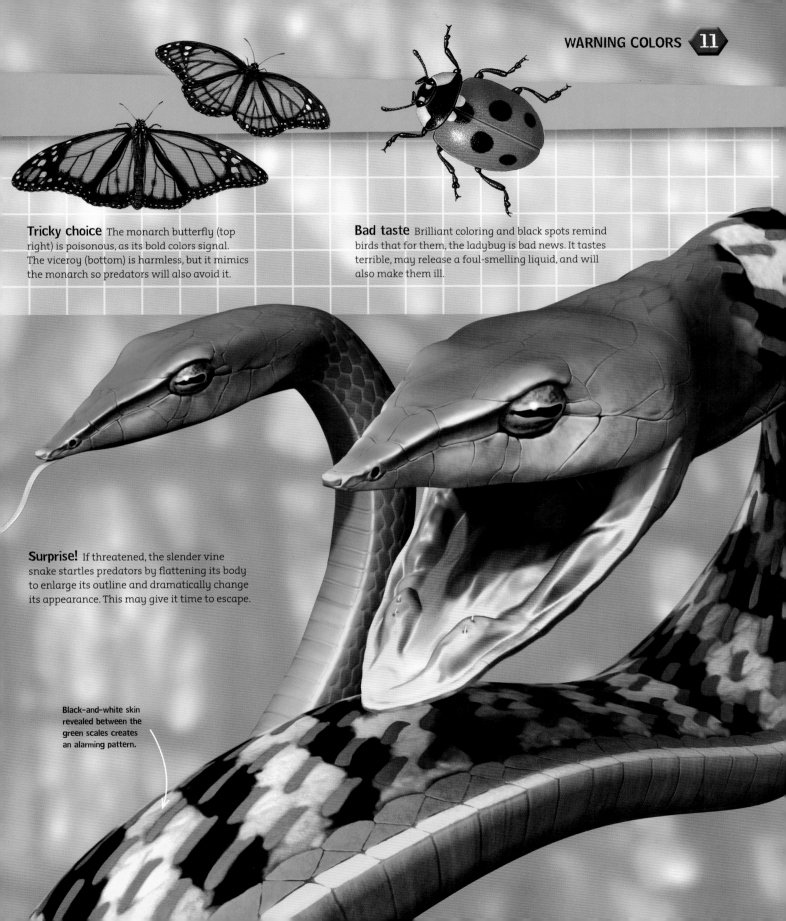

Tricky choice The monarch butterfly (top right) is poisonous, as its bold colors signal. The viceroy (bottom) is harmless, but it mimics the monarch so predators will also avoid it.

Bad taste Brilliant coloring and black spots remind birds that for them, the ladybug is bad news. It tastes terrible, may release a foul-smelling liquid, and will also make them ill.

Surprise! If threatened, the slender vine snake startles predators by flattening its body to enlarge its outline and dramatically change its appearance. This may give it time to escape.

Black-and-white skin revealed between the green scales creates an alarming pattern.

Black and white

The combination of black and white is a common form of camouflage. Bands and stripes break up the outline of the body, and that confuses predators. These colors also help animals blend in with shadows. Black may be used to regulate body temperature, too, as it soaks up the sun better than pale colors.

Quick change The magpie's black-and-white coloring is highly conspicuous in the open, but when it seeks the shelter of trees, its markings can look like splashes of sunlight in the leaves.

Black is best for absorbing heat from the sun.

Peaceful bear

As a symbol of the conservation movement, China's giant panda is one of the most recognizable of animals. Sadly, this gentle, bamboo-eating bear is threatened by the clearing of its mountain forests and is poached for its striking black-and-white coat.

Black patches enlarge the panda's small dark eyes, making the stare it gives an opponent seem more threatening.

Dual purpose For predators from above, the penguin's black back is hard to distinguish from the water. For unsuspecting fish below, its white front blends in with the light from the sky.

Animal facts

❶ The largest polar predators, orcas, or killer whales, share the same black-and-white camouflage as the penguins they prey on.

❷ Australian swans are jet black, while their cousins in the Northern Hemisphere are pure white.

❸ The black-and-white markings of a skunk are a signal to predators that it is a meal best avoided.

Hidden hunter Shadows provide the perfect cover for the pied kingfisher; even its watchful eyes are masked. It waits motionless until it spies a fish, then dives to skewer it with its sharp bill.

Stealthy predator The snowy owl is difficult to detect when it swoops over the tundra in search of prey. For protection from the cold, its legs and feet are also covered in white feathers.

Beware! Pipevine swallowtail caterpillars feed on poisonous plants, and the toxins remain in the body of the adult butterfly. The butterfly's black-and-white markings warn birds of this.

Stripes The zebra's distinctive stripes come in different patterns and widths and, like human fingerprints, are unique to each animal. The stripes help individuals identify one another.

The zebra's mane hair is short, neat, and upright, unlike that of its relative, the horse.

Blue morpho
butterfly

Spotlight on

Tails Members of the swallowtail family of butterflies are found in most parts of the world. These large butterflies are fast and powerful fliers. They get their name from the long "tail" on each wing.

butterflies

Most butterflies fly by day. Their brilliant coloring does not come from pigments, but from rows of tiny scales that cover their wings. These reflect sunlight in a special way to produce glittering patterns. Unlike caterpillars, butterflies have a liquid-only diet, such as nectar, which they suck up through their long, tubelike tongue.

Caterpillar sheds
outer skin.

Opaque chrysalis

Breaking out

Wet and
crumpled

Blood is pumped
into wings.

Wings dry
and harden.

Monarch is
ready to fly.

Making of a monarch butterfly

During its time in the chrysalis, the body parts of the caterpillar break down and adult features grow in their place. The chrysalis becomes transparent as the transformation progresses.

Butterflies have a knob on the end of each long, thin antenna. Moths do not.

By suddenly opening its wings, this butterfly reveals two eye-shaped spots. They are a trick to confuse predators.

The map butterfly has two different forms. The one that emerges in spring is shown here. Those emerging in summer are black and white.

Butterflies rest with their wings folded up over their back. This eighty-eight butterfly is named for the pattern on its outer wings.

Sun lover This South American butterfly basks with its wings open while sucking on liquid nectar. The undersides of its wings are surprisingly drab, making it inconspicuous when it rests with its wings closed.

Making light

Animals that are active at night, such as fireflies, and creatures that live in the dark ocean depths cannot use color to send signals. Instead, some use chemicals in their body to produce light, which they beam out to communicate. Light is used to attract a mate, to fend off attack, and to locate or lure food.

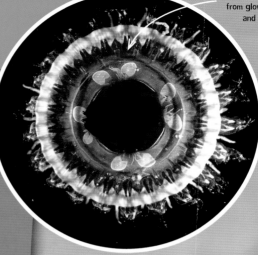

In some parts of the deep ocean, the main source of light comes from glowing animals and not the sun.

Flashlights Deep-sea jellyfish are usually dark colored. When threatened, some pump out circles of bright blue light, like a flashing burglar alarm. The attacker flees, fearful that the glow will attract an even larger predator.

Coded signals The flashing lights of male fireflies are courtship signals. Females recognize the unique flashing patterns of their own species and answer with their own light signals.

Chemical substances mix in the abdomen to make the glow. This is called "cold light"—that is, all light and no heat.

Soft light The glowing long outer tentacles of the tube anemone startle fish that may be tempted to take a bite. These food-gathering tools are also armed with stings.

The bright beam attracts predators hunting for food. But instead of eating, they will become the meal.

Do undersea animals send out light in all colors?

Light work The deep-sea anglerfish waits for prey lured by the light that dangles near its gaping mouth. Backward-curving teeth make sure that nothing it catches can escape. Prey is swallowed whole, not chewed.

Rattail fish live in the inky blackness of the deep ocean. They have light-producing organs underneath the skin of their abdomen.

Sea pen

The quill-like sea pen flashes bright green light when touched.

A: No, most make only blue and green light, as it can be seen better in seawater.

Changing colors

Some animals are able to quickly change color to either confuse an attacker or to hide by blending into the background. Some change colors to show their mood, to threaten an enemy perhaps, or to attract a mate. Others change with the temperature or with the season. For some, changing colors is simply a matter of age.

What fish turns red as it moves from the ocean into freshwater?

Dressed for the season

In winter, birds and mammals of the Arctic tundra grow thick white coats of fur or feathers, both for warmth and as camouflage in the snow. In spring, these are replaced with thinner coats of brownish gray, which match the colors of the summer landscape.

The feathers of the willow ptarmigan become thicker in winter and turn from brown to pure white.

Summer

Summer

Winter

Winter

In the far north, the arctic hare is white all year. Farther south they are brown during the summer.

Each eye can swivel independently to look in different directions at the same time.

Color signal The male panther chameleon can turn from calm blue-green to angry red to intimidate rivals. Three layers of pigments under its transparent skin work together to make different colors.

Tri-colored These three coiled snakes are all green tree pythons. The young are either brick brown or bright yellow when they hatch. They become the lime green of adults in one to three years.

In the early morning, the lizard is still cold and cannot run quickly to escape predators.

Solar powered Reptiles need heat from the sun for energy. As it basks on warm rocks, this agama lizard changes color throughout the day. The stronger colors match its increased energy level.

By late morning, its vivid body colors are a sign to predators that it will be hard to catch.

ZOOM IN

Rapid response
Cuttlefish react to danger by immediately changing their color to match their surroundings. They can take on the mottled shades of the seafloor in just seconds.

A: Sockeye salmon, returning to spawn in the streams where they were born.

See-through

For fragile creatures not protected by shells, speed, or toxins, transparency is the perfect defense technique. Predators literally see right through them, allowing delicate animals to survive in dangerous environments. Equally, it also allows transparent hunters, such as some jellyfish, to remain unseen as they stalk or lure prey.

The eyes have it The dark eyes of this juvenile squid gleam like black marbles from its tiny and nearly translucent body. The stomach, because of its contents, is also visible.

Clear skin Glass frogs are small tree dwellers, with most species no more than 1 inch (2.5 cm) long. While the skin color of most glass frogs is green, some members of this family lack pigment on their abdomen.

Nothing to hide

The thick, elastic substance that forms the body, or "bell," of a jellyfish is 95 percent water. Jellyfish have no brain, heart, or bones, and mostly, no eyes. Tentacles deliver food trapped on the sticky bell to the mouth. Jellyfish move by opening and closing the bell.

The four rings seen here are reproductive organs. In the center is the mouth, a single opening where food enters and waste leaves.

Animal facts

1 The Portuguese man-of-war has a transparent body but colorful stingers that look like baby fish.

2 Young flounder are transparent and also have a flat, thin body, making them almost impossible to see when you are looking at them from the side.

3 The larvae of many fish, such as eels and herring, are transparent.

Tiny and transparent

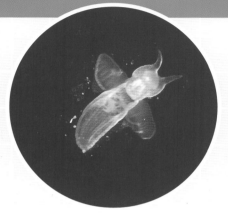

Disappearing act Many small deep-sea creatures, such as this bristleworm from icy Antarctic waters, have a transparent body that makes them virtually invisible.

Water wings Although it does not have a shell, the naked sea butterfly is a mollusk and is related to snails and clams. It is propelled by finlike extensions on its feet, which look like wings.

Whale food Shrimplike krill spend the day in the ocean depths, but at night gather in swarms to feed on the surface, where they are scooped up in great mouthfuls by baleen whales.

The internal organs, including the heart, can be easily seen through the translucent skin.

Bare beauty Glasswing butterflies lack the color-producing scales that give other butterflies their brilliant markings. This allows the background to show through their wings, making them less visible.

The colorless tissue between the veins in the wings looks like clear glass.

Dressed to impress

In the breeding season, males use decorations, such as bold colors and long tails, or displays of singing or dancing to gain the attention of females. Males with the best markings or ability to perform have the most success in finding mates and therefore in producing more offspring.

Ranked by color The brilliant red and blue of this mandrill indicates that it is a mature male. The male also has a yellow beard and the color of his naked rump can range from blue to purple.

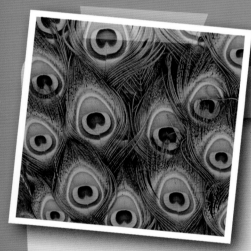

The peacock uses muscles in his tail to spread out his magnificent feathers. He can also shake the feathers so they rattle.

Pick me!

With his shimmering feathers arched into a fabulous fan, the peacock dances and struts to impress peahens. Peahens choose the male with the most elaborately patterned feathers. Successful males acquire a harem of up to five peahens.

After the breeding season is over, the tail feathers fall out but are rapidly regrown the following year.

Peahen

 ## Animal facts

1 The brilliant colors on the big bills of puffins are brightest during the breeding season.

2 After breeding, the male wood duck sheds his ornate plumage and takes on the drabber colors of the female.

3 When the male three-spined stickleback fish needs to attract a mate, it develops a deep red chest and throat and bright blue eyes.

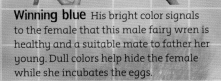

Winning blue His bright color signals to the female that this male fairy wren is healthy and a suitable mate to father her young. Dull colors help hide the female while she incubates the eggs.

Glowing reports The red plumage of the male northern cardinal comes from pigments in the seeds it eats. The best foragers develop the deepest colors, a sign to females of their ability to provide.

Pumped The male frigate bird has a pouch of brilliant red skin in his throat, which he blows up like a balloon to attract a mate. He keeps it inflated until joined by a female.

When angry or excited, the blue color of the mandrill's buttocks becomes more intense.

LAND, AIR, AND SEA

The incredible variety of animal life on our planet is reflected in the many clever ways they have developed to live in all conditions and situations, to communicate, to hunt for food, and to protect themselves and their young. From sightless fish in the ocean depths to soaring sharp-eyed eagles, all have extraordinary skills.

A family of giraffes treks across the grasslands.

Scare tactics

Fighting takes time and energy and can result in injury or death. To avoid physical combat, many animals use signals and body tricks to deter attackers or rivals. These threat displays include emphasizing their size by raising their hair or standing side on; showing off weapons, such as teeth; and other facial expressions.

Tiny terror House wrens are spirited and aggressive, and despite their tiny size, boldly defend their territory with a menacing display of bristling feathers, outstretched wings, and fanned tail.

Back off! The raised hairs on the back of the neck, snarling lip curled back to show sharp teeth, intent stare, and tail held stiff and upright are all signals that this gray wolf is ready to attack.

The blue-tongued skink surprises attackers by poking out its alarmingly colored tongue.

Bluffing birds

Creating a distraction To defend their chicks, ostriches run toward the attacker with beating wings, dodge out of reach, then repeat the performance. The chicks slip away in the confusion.

Animal facts

1 To discourage a potential attacker, elephants stand tall and spread their flapping ears wide to make their bulky outline look even more imposing.

2 Frilled lizards spread their frill to suddenly seem larger.

3 Cats arch upright and raise their hair to increase their body outline.

Read my lips The open-mouthed yawn of the hippopotamus has nothing to do with tiredness. Instead it is a threatening gesture, designed to display the dangerous tusks it uses in battles for mating rights.

Making a noise

When animals shriek, croak, bark, howl, or squawk, they are sending a clear message. Some of the loudest calls are made by males during the breeding season, either to attract a mate or to scare away a rival. Other calls warn of danger, threaten intruders, or, sometimes, tell others of the group where there is food or water.

Bursts of sound To warn off rival males, the black rhinoceros blasts out a low growl, which is mostly below the range of human hearing. Rhinos also make a high-pitched squeak and a mooing sound.

Mating call The bullfrog gets its name from the deep, loud call of the male, which resembles the bellow of a bull. The calls are noisiest on warm nights during the breeding season.

Stag

Animal facts

1 The lion's roar is the loudest sound cats can make.

2 Cicadas can produce a noise as loud as a power saw. Some can be heard from ¼ mile (400 m) away.

3 Rattlesnakes have dried scales on their tail, which they shake to make a rattle.

Stags have bellowing **contests** to show their fitness and endurance.

Alarm call These howler monkeys are screaming a danger warning to a member of their group. They also howl to tell other groups to stay away. These are the noisiest animals on land.

Rumble and roar
Elephants communicate with deep rumbling sounds that they can detect up to 2 miles (3.2 km) away. When excited or angry, they blow air through their trunk to produce a loud, trumpeting call.

Spotlight on

hummingbirds

The male Anna's hummingbird grows to 4 inches (10 cm) long.

Hummingbirds live in the Americas and the Caribbean. They are known for their tiny size, their brilliant coloring, and their amazing agility in flight. They are the only birds that can truly hover in midair, with their wings a blur of movement as they stay in position to collect nectar from flowers. They are also capable of backward flight.

Rufous hummingbirds feed on long, tube-shaped flowers that are the perfect shape to fit their bill.

A female collects silky plant fibers to line her nest.

The mother feeds nectar and partly digested insects to her rapidly growing chicks.

Nesting

Tiny, cup-shaped nests woven from moss and lichen are anchored in the fork of a twig or to the underside of a leaf. The nest is bound with spider's web, which allows it to expand as the chicks grow.

The hummingbird dips its long, thin bill into a flower to lick up nectar with its brush-tipped tongue.

High energy To fuel their vigorous flying, hummingbirds feed on energy-rich nectar, selecting flowers with the highest sugar content. Small insects add protein to their diet. They eat more than their own weight each day.

Rufous hummingbird

Aerial display With rapidly beating wings, a male hummingbird hovers in front of a female, turning his head from side to side to flash his shimmering neck feathers.

Chatterbox All hummingbirds buzz, call, and chirp to defend their feeding territory. Anna's hummingbirds make more noises for a longer period of time than other hummingbirds.

Aerial acrobatics

Birds are masters of the skies, swooping, soaring, and hovering in fantastic displays of flying skills. But they are not the only airborne performers. Although bats are the only mammals with wings, other mammals, such as squirrels, as well as some reptiles, use stretched flaps of skin to glide through the air.

Falcons dive to strike and take prey in midair.

Dancing on air Many birds of prey, such as these marsh harriers, put on a twisting and tumbling double act. The movements of the pair are perfectly coordinated.

Male

The male is dropping a gift of food into the waiting claws of the upside-down female.

Female

Handy wings Bats are the only mammals that fly like birds. A bat's wing has the same structure as an arm and hand, with webs of thin skin between each long finger.

Can fish fly?

The long furry tail is used to steer and to slow down.

Energy efficient The skin flaps between the outstretched limbs of the gliding squirrel act like a parachute, allowing it to glide gently from tree to tree. This is easier than climbing up and down.

Animal facts

1 Courting African fish-eagles perform midair cartwheels with their feet hooked together.

2 Condors reach great heights by riding upward on rising currents of warm air.

3 Gannets plunge beak-first into water to spear fish. Their eyes are at the front of the head and point forward. This overlapping field of view helps the birds pinpoint prey.

Flocks of starlings **take off,** fly, and come in to roost as one.

A: *Yes, some fish have broad, winglike fins that help them shoot over the water when escaping predators.*

Everyday living

Over time, all animals have developed helpful attributes to improve their chances of finding food and staying safe. Some have extraordinary speed to chase prey or flee from attack or use strong hind limbs to leap from danger. Others have powerful beaks to pierce tough-shelled fruits. Each creature adapts to its own location.

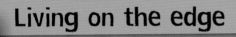

Living on the edge

Mountain goats live on the snow-covered alps of North America, choosing the highest outcrops and the steepest slopes where predators cannot reach them. Their hooves can spread wide and have a gripping, almost rubber-like inner pad. This helps them balance and find footholds on slippery rocks.

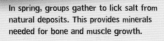

In spring, groups gather to lick salt from natural deposits. This provides minerals needed for bone and muscle growth.

Mountain goats move between clifftop resting places and can leap nearly 12 feet (3.6 m) in a single bound.

What is the fastest creature in the air?

Running on water The basilisk lizard has large, fringed scales on its toes that act like paddles and make it possible for it to scamper at high speed across the surface of the water.

Animal facts

1 Many lizards can drop their tail, which will keep wriggling to distract the attacker while the lizard escapes. It then grows a new tail.

2 The mole has shovel-like front paws and a strong sense of smell for a life of digging through soil searching for worms.

3 The cheetah is the fastest animal on land, able to reach 45 miles (72 km) per hour, but it hunts in short bursts only.

A taste for heights Using its long, muscular tongue, the giraffe grasps branches and pulls leaves into its mouth. It can extend its tongue up to 18 inches (46 cm). Thick saliva helps protect its mouth from thorns.

Mountain gorilla

Chest-thumping gorillas look **fearsome**, but they seldom fight.

A: *The peregrine falcon. Its dive speed to catch a bird in flight can be more than 200 miles (322 km) per hour.*

Spikes and shells

Under the sea

Small animals are not fast enough to escape a predator, or strong enough to fight back. So they use armor to protect their soft body from attack. Many sea creatures, and land animals such as snails and turtles, have hard shells to hide in. Others, such as porcupines and the Australian echidna, defend themselves with spikes and prickly coats.

Strong armor This shell protects the soft body of a mollusk. The projecting prongs are used to protect it from predators.

Are hedgehogs born with spines?

Well equipped The thorny devil of central Australia is well adapted to desert life—the spikes protect it from predators and the pattern of scales on its body channels dew and rainwater into its mouth.

Animal facts

1 One species of armadillo can curl into a completely enclosed ball, so that it presents only the hard plates of its back and head to an attacker.

2 When alarmed, the echidna burrows quickly into soft earth until only the tops of its spikes are visible.

3 Lobsters are protected by hard, overlapping rings of cuticle, like the armor of a medieval knight.

Hard plates of **horny skin** shield the head and back of the armadillo.

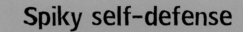

Ready to wear Unlike other crabs, the hermit crab does not have a hard outer covering, so it finds an empty shell to live in. The flowery anemones on the top of the shell provide further protection.

Prickly The sea urchin defends itself with long, sharp spines that sometimes contain poison. The spines also help it move about on the seafloor. They grow from the hard shell that encases the animal's body.

Puffed up By swallowing water into a stomach pouch, the porcupine fish swells like a balloon. This forces its spines upright. When the danger passes, the fish slowly deflates and the spines lie flat.

Spiky self-defense

If threatened, the porcupine turns its back, raises its spines, and charges backward into its attacker. Some spines come off and stay stuck in the enemy. The hedgehog curls into a tight ball, making a prickly mouthful for would-be predators.

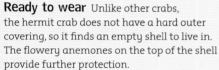

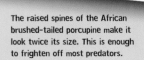

The raised spines of the African brushed-tailed porcupine make it look twice its size. This is enough to frighten off most predators.

When fully rolled, the hedgehog's spines protect its head and soft body. It does not have spines on the underside of its body.

A: Yes, but they are soft and rubbery. They do not pop up until the baby hedgehog is a few hours old.

COURTSHIP AND MATING

The purpose of every animal's life is to produce more of its own kind. Nearly every species uses some kind of signal to attract a mate. Then, in many species, elaborate rituals of singing, dancing, and other displays of fitness follow, to allow the female to choose the best father for her young.

A peacock raises and shakes his spectacular tail as a courtship display.

Finding a mate

Each species has its own way of locating and luring a mate. Many animals use visual signals, with males developing colorful fur, feathers, or scales at the start of each breeding season. Others use sound—birds and insects sing and chirp coded calls. Some creatures release special scents or offer gifts.

Gifts The male kingfisher brings the female small fish. If she declines the offering, he eats it himself. He may have to repeat this performance several times before she accepts.

Wins by a nose At the start of the breeding season, mature male elephant seals fight for females. By inflating their nose they make drumlike sounds to warn lesser males away.

The male **emperor moth** has the best sense of smell of any animal.

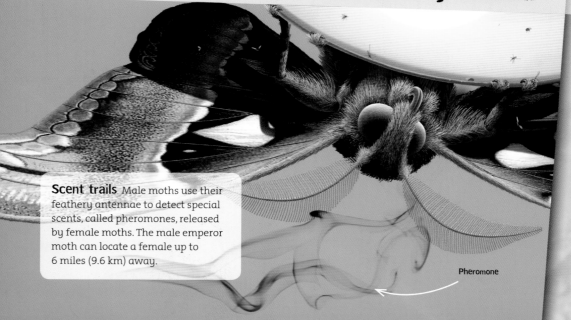

Scent trails Male moths use their feathery antennae to detect special scents, called pheromones, released by female moths. The male emperor moth can locate a female up to 6 miles (9.6 km) away.

Calling for a mate Only male frogs croak—both to attract a female and to warn other males to stay away. An inflated pouch of air in the frog's mouth makes the sound louder.

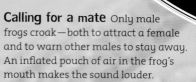
Pheromone

Power play To defend his territory the male Siamese fighting fish intimidates rivals with flared gill covers and outspread fins. He may use the same aggressive display in his pursuit of a female.

Male

Female

Cautious approach The tiny male orb-weaver spider strums a special mating signal from the edge of the female's web to make sure she does not mistake him for prey.

Spotlight on

Making contact A male cricket chirps by rubbing a "file" on one of his front wings against a scraper on the other. Other crickets pick up the messages using hearing organs on their abdomen.

The loudest noisemakers, such as this well-camouflaged green bush cricket, are usually the ones that are hardest to see.

sounds and signals

Male crickets, katydids, and grasshoppers "sing" by rubbing two parts of their body together. Each species has its own unique series of chirps, and the females reply only to males of their own species. There are three types of song—one to call a female closer, one to persuade her to mate, and a battle call warning off other males.

Summer nights Unlike grasshoppers and cicadas, crickets and katydids, such as this leaf katydid, call only at dusk or at night, never during the day. The frequency of their chirps increases with the temperature.

Ready for action Cicada nymphs emerge from underground in midsummer and climb the nearest tree to shed their casing. Males then begin broadcasting their loud call to find females.

The Jerusalem cricket spends most of its life below ground where it drums out signals by beating its body against the earth.

The field cricket lives in grassy meadows. The loud call of the male finds females and warns off other males.

Serenade Male grasshoppers, such as this painted grasshopper, produce calls by rapidly rubbing a rough "file" on the inside of their back legs against hard ridges on the edge of their wings.

Birdsong

During the breeding season, many male birds sing to attract a mate and to threaten rivals. The order of high and low notes, and the pauses between each part of the song, are unique to each species. This lets females recognize the correct males. Young males learn songs of their species by copying their father.

The bird's tail resembles a lyre—a stringed instrument like a small harp.

Performer The male lyrebird dances with its filmy tail fanned over his head. At the same time he sends out his own rasping call as well as a mixture of expertly mimicked local birdsongs and other sounds.

Animal facts

1 Calls to warn of danger and to make contact are shorter and not as musical as the male's courting song.

2 Some birds stop singing when they find a mate and do not sing again until the next breeding season.

3 Songbirds are often small and drab, but they make up for this with loud and elaborate songs.

Family chorus The call of the kookaburra moves from a low chuckle to a full-throated cackle and back to a chuckle. Kookaburras live in large family groups and all "laugh" together.

Kookaburras call in the early morning and at dusk.

Mixed messages Willow ptarmigans live in the frozen north. As spring approaches, males scream a warning to other males to stay off their territory. They send a quickly repeated croaking to entice females.

Seasonal songs Robins, both male and female, warble sad, flutelike songs from their separate winter territories. As the weather warms, they change to cheerier tunes and the females join the males to mate.

Love song At the start of the breeding season, the male horned owl calls the female to his territory with low hoots. The courtship continues with the male and female singing to each other.

The male common yellowthroat pours out its song at sunrise.

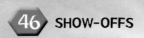

Listen and look Dolphins communicate underwater with whistles, squeaks, and clicking calls. They leap above the waves to impress mates, to let other dolphins know where they are, or just for fun.

Undersea communication

Whales and dolphins send messages to others of their species using a variety of underwater calls. This helps to keep traveling groups together, to coordinate their movements when hunting prey, and to warn each other of danger. The way they leap, or slap the water with their flippers and tail, also carries meaning.

 Animal facts

● When a whale's tail slaps loudly on the water it may mean "stay away."

● Dusky dolphins leap to show they have found a school of fish and need the group to gather and cooperate in hunting them.

● The beluga whale is called the sea canary because of its chirping, clicking, and whistling.

Humpback whale

Male humpbacks "sing" long and complex songs that can be heard hundreds of miles away.

Messaging Humpback whales may leap from the water more than a hundred times in a row. Called breaching, this seems to be a way of sending signals to other humpbacks.

Underwater chorus Male leopard toadfish make a tooting sound, called a boat whistle, to attract females. They call in a pattern. When one male toots, nearby males grunt.

Fighting for a mate

In most species, males must compete with other males for access to females. Many males have developed weapons, such as horns and antlers. The largest and strongest succeed and breed. In some mammal species males control a group of females and must frequently fight off rivals who try to steal them.

Are male kangaroos the only boxing animals?

Fighting tools and techniques

Males push, wrestle, batter, stab, kick, and bite in the contest to win the right to mate. Horses and zebras lash out with hard, sharp-edged hooves. Male jungle fowl spar with razor-sharp spurs. Male creatures from beetles to buffaloes battle rivals with horns.

Giraffes establish rank with neck-wrestling contests. They intertwine their necks, then push until one gives way. Those with the strongest necks are most successful and therefore father more young.

Zebras live in groups of several mares dominated by a single stallion. The stallion defends his harem from the attentions of other stallions by biting and kicking.

Boxing kangaroos
Male kangaroos battle by grabbing and jabbing with their short front legs and kicking with their powerful back legs. To win, one male must push the other to the ground.

Animal facts

1 Rival rattlesnakes could kill each other but keep their mouth shut to avoid this. Instead they bump and wrestle until one gives up and leaves.

2 Each breeding season, male deer grow impressive antlers to fight off rivals and win females. The antlers are shed in fall.

3 Male mountain sheep noisily and repeatedly crash their heavy horns headfirst into each other until one gives up.

Siberian tigers

Tigers **fight fiercely** to drive rival males off their territory.

A: No, male hares compete for females by boxing.

Spotlight on

These Hercules beetles from Peru grow to 4 inches (10 cm) long.

giant beetles

Mighty beetles are found in rainforests around the world. The heaviest is the Goliath beetle, from Africa, which weighs up to 4 ounces (113 g), and the largest is the male Hercules beetle, from Central America, which grows to more than 7 inches (18 cm) long. Males are armed with massive horns that are sometimes longer than their body.

Forest recycler
Larvae of the Southeast Asian Atlas beetle feed on decaying logs on the rainforest floor. The size of their adult horns depends on the quality of the food they eat in the immature stage.

Locking horns Competing male Hercules beetles wrestle with their huge horns. These fights look ferocious but rarely result in serious injury. The winner claims the territory and the waiting female.

The female Hercules beetle does not have horns.

Well built The forward-pointing horns of the elephant beetle resemble tusks. Like all giant beetles, it is very strong for its size. Some can lift more than 300 times their own weight.

Battle-ready The horns of the male stag beetle are actually enlarged jaws. They look like the antlers of a deer and are used for the same purpose—pushing and butting in contests of strength with rivals.

Showy feathers

Some of the most elaborate feather arrangements are found on male birds of paradise in the New Guinea rainforest. Their showy feathers are used in the courting ritual and are on the most visible parts of the body—brilliant patches of crimson and sapphire on the breast and upper wings, and long, cascading tails.

How do birds replace old or damaged feathers?

Crowning glory

In many species, both the male and the female sport showy headwear. Some wear permanent crowns of feathers, while others have colorful crests that can be raised and lowered at will to communicate with others of their own species or to frighten off an intruder.

The sulfur-crested cockatoo of Australia raises its forward-curving crest into a broad crown when it is startled or excited.

The Victoria crowned pigeon of the New Guinea rainforests wears a crest of filmy feathers. It is the world's largest living pigeon.

The crowned crane lives on the African grasslands, where it prances, jumps, and bows with its pom-pom headdress of stiff, golden feathers.

Show time Using its strong feet to perch, the Raggiana bird of paradise sets its tail feathers quivering to show off its striking colors. Groups of competing males perform together, each trying to win the female.

Acrobatic display Hanging upside down, the blue bird of paradise fluffs its breast feathers, spreads its wings, and shows off its two black tail plumes.

A: At least once a year birds gradually lose all their feathers and grow new ones.

Elaborate dances

Dancing as a part of courtship is most common in the bird world. In many species, the male dances for the female, while she watches and judges. In other species, both partners perform. Moves always follow the same pattern and can include intricate stepping and jumping, flapping outstretched wings, nodding, and swaying together.

Underwater ballet The sea horse straightens its tail to rise and curls it to sink. Courting pairs often twist their tails together. After mating, the male carries the eggs in his pouch.

Penguin pairs recognize each other by their distinct calls.

Annual dance Macaroni penguins reunite with their partners each spring at their nesting site. The female arrives later than the male, who welcomes her by bowing, stretching out his flippers, and waving his head from side to side.

Animal facts

1 Pairs of western grebes perform synchronized dances on top of the water. Each holds a long strand of water weed in its bill.

2 The male stickleback fish zigzags back and forth in front of the female, who then follows him to his nest.

3 The male blue-footed booby stamps his impressive blue feet and flaps his wings.

The male **fiddler crab** darts back and forth waving his large, colored claw.

Mates for life Cape gannets breed off the coast of southern Africa. Each year when pairs return to their nesting sites they greet each other with necks stretched upward, then dance together to re-establish their bond.

Which birds build a stage to dance on?

A: *Lyrebirds and bowerbirds.*

Courtship rituals

In many species, once a male has caught the attention of a potential mate, he must then convince her of his fitness to father healthy young. This may involve performing a set of physical feats, such as energetic dancing, acrobatic flying, or showing off hunting skills or homemaking skills.

Face touching can continue for days before mating takes place.

Gentle persuasion The male North American freshwater turtle swims toward the female, then strokes her face with his oversized front claws. She may pat his forelimbs in reply.

Monkeys grooming

Animal facts

1 The blue-footed booby impresses prospective mates with his bright webbed feet. Females choose males with the bluest feet.

2 The male wolf spider signals to the female by waving his front legs and shaking his abdomen. She may respond by attacking him.

3 The tree squirrel chases his chosen mate along tree branches. If she gets too far ahead, she stops and waits for him.

Monkeys build **deep bonds** by grooming each other.

Strong vibes To impress females and frighten rivals, male alligators make a deep rumble, like silent purring, then bellow loudly. Vibrations from these sounds send bubbles and ripples to the surface.

The shimmering water makes the male more noticeable to other alligators.

Master fisher The male kingfisher demonstrates his fishing skill by diving headfirst into the water to spear a fish with his dagger-like bill. He will feed his catch to the female.

Spotlight on

MacGregor's bowerbird

bowerbirds

Bowerbirds live in Australia and New Guinea. Males build intricate structures of sticks, not as nests, but simply to impress females. Colored ornaments surround a dancing platform at the front. The female inspects and compares bowers and chooses to mate with the male whose bower is most solidly built and best decorated.

Display homes

Cones and corridors Bower design varies from species to species. There are two main forms—the maypole-shaped structure of gardener bowerbirds (right) and arched avenues such as that of the satin bowerbird (far right).

Skilled architects The large, hutlike structure of the Vogelkop gardener bowerbird is the most elaborate of all. The male spends most of the year tending it and rearranging the decorations.

Fixing up

Most male bowerbirds have fairly drab plumage, and rely instead on their building and decorating skills to attract females. Those species with brighter coloring, such as the regent bowerbird, spend less time building bowers but back up their simpler structures with a display of fine feathers.

The male regent bowerbird flicks open his wings to show off a band of glossy gold. He also offers decorations from his small bower.

In addition to his carefully tended bower, the male great bowerbird can impress females with his lilac crest.

Gardener bowerbirds pile twigs around the stem of a small tree then decorate their handiwork with flowers and fruits.

The satin bowerbird favors blue ornaments—bottlecaps, feathers, and pieces of glass. He often steals items from the bowers of rivals.

After mating, the female works alone to build a separate nest for the eggs. The male continues courting other females.

Gift giving

Many male birds bring food to the females as evidence of their ability to provide for chicks and to give the female nourishment while she produces and incubates the eggs. Some offer nesting material. For insect predators such as some spiders and flies, the female is distracted with a gift of food so that she does not attack the male as prey.

Building a bond The male great blue heron gathers large twigs, which he presents to the female with much bowing and head shaking. She uses them to build their platform-like nest.

Bridal meal To make sure she does not eat him, the male nursery web spider presents the female with a meal of dead insect, wrapped in silk. Mating takes place while she dines.

The male spider gift wraps his offering in silk.

How long does it take
a weaver bird to build
its nest?

?

Weavers breed in
large groups, so many
males build nests in
the same tree.

It is difficult for predators
to approach and enter
the hanging nest's
narrow entrance.

Homemaker The male black-headed weaver
builds a secure nest by knotting and weaving
together grass and strips of leaf. The female
then inspects his handiwork, and if she is
happy with it, moves in.

🐾 Animal facts

❶ A cormorant arriving to relieve its
mate sitting on the eggs must bring a
gift of seaweed or it will be driven away.

❷ The male praying mantis offers himself
as a gift. After mating, he is eaten by the
female, and his body provides protein for
the developing eggs.

❸ Male balloon flies give pretty, but empty,
silken packages to the female.

A: *Two to three days.*

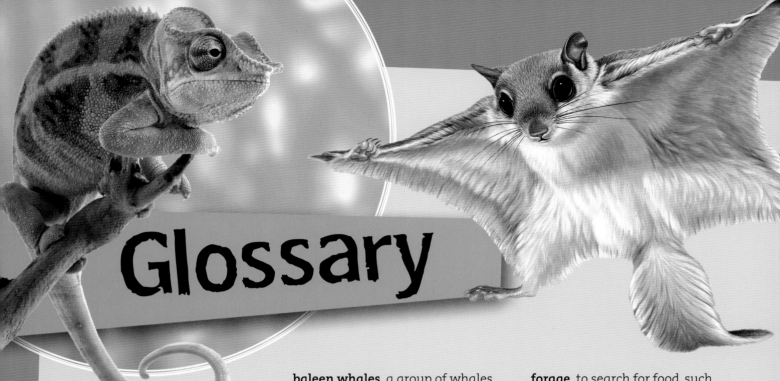

Glossary

abdomen the part of an animal's body that contains the digestive system and organs of reproduction

adapt to change in order to survive in certain conditions. This usually takes place over many generations.

algae the simplest forms of plant life. Algae do not have true stems, roots, or leaves. Most are found in water.

Antarctic the very cold region near the South Pole

antenna a delicate sense organ on the head of an insect, sometimes called a feeler, which it uses to smell, touch, or hear the world

antlers bony growths on the heads of some male animals, such as deer, elk, and moose. Antlers grow and are shed each year.

Arctic the very cold region near the North Pole

baleen whales a group of whales that instead of teeth have comblike plates, also called whalebone, that are used to filter food out of seawater

bask to sit in the sun in order to increase body temperature

breeding season the time of the year when birds and animals find mates and produce young. For many animals, the breeding season is spring.

camouflage body colors, patterns, or shapes that help an animal blend in with and stay hidden in its natural surroundings

caterpillar the larva of a moth or butterfly

chrysalis the protective casing a caterpillar lives in while it turns into a butterfly or moth

courtship the process of attracting a mate

display a series of actions that send signals to attract mates or to frighten off rivals and possible attackers

forage to search for food, such as seeds or fruits

frill a collar around a frilled lizard's neck. It can be raised to surprise a predator.

gill the organ that sea-living creatures, such as fish, use to get oxygen from the water

groom to clean and care for the skin and fur. Grooming can be done by the animal itself or by one animal for another.

harem a collection of female animals that are under the control of a single male

incubate to protect and keep eggs at the right temperature by sitting on them or placing them in nests. This allows the young to develop and hatch.

juvenile a young animal that does not have the markings or plumage of the adult

krill tiny, shrimplike sea creatures that live in large numbers in Arctic and Antarctic waters

larva the young stage of an insect, when it looks very different from its parents. The larva undergoes a total change, called complete metamorphosis, to reach the adult form. Caterpillars and grubs are larvae.

mammals a group of animals that have hair or fur, are warm-blooded, and feed their young with milk

mate one of a pair of animals that produce young together

mollusk an animal, such as a snail or oyster, with no backbone and a soft body that is usually enclosed or partly enclosed in a shell

nectar a sweet liquid produced in the flowers of many plants in order to attract insects and birds who then transfer seeds to other plants

organ a part of the body that has a special function, such as the heart or the liver

pheromone a chemical released by one animal that sends a message to others of the same species. Many insects use pheromones to attract a mate.

pigment the material in living tissue that gives it color

plumage a bird's entire covering of feathers

pores tiny openings in the skin

predator an animal that survives by hunting, killing, and eating other animals

prey an animal or animals that are hunted, killed, and eaten by other animals

rainforest a forest that receives at least 100 inches (2,540 mm) of rainfall each year. Most rainforests are in tropical regions.

rival an animal that competes with another for food, territory, or a mate

spawn to lay a mass of eggs directly into the water, as fish, frogs, and many other water creatures do

species a group of animals that have certain features in common. Members of a species are able to breed with one another and produce young.

spines long, sharp structures that can pierce flesh and, sometimes, inject poison

spurs sharp, clawlike structures on the legs of some birds and mammals

tentacle a slender, flexible feeler that enables an animal without a backbone, such as a mollusk, to feel and grasp things and, sometimes, to inject poison

territory the area that an animal or group of animals of the same species uses for feeding and breeding

toxin a poisonous substance produced by an animal or plant that is harmful to other animals or to humans

tropical describes the hot regions close to the equator

tundra in Arctic regions, a huge, frozen, and mostly flat area where no trees grow

tusk the very long, pointed tooth on either side of the mouth of some animals, such as the elephant and the hippopotamus

wingspan the widest distance between the tip of one wing and the tip of the other wing on a bird, bat, or insect

Index

A
African brush-tailed porcupines, 37
African fish-eagles, 33
agama lizards, 19
alligators, 56–57
anglerfish, 17
Anna's hummingbirds, 30, 31
antlers, 49
arctic hares, 18
armadillos, 36
Atlas beetles, 50
Australian pineapple fish, 8

B
baleen whales, 21
balloon flies, 61
basilisk lizards, 34–35
bats, 32
beluga whales, 46
birds of paradise, 52–53
black-headed weaver birds, 61
black rhinoceroses, 28
blue-banded gobies, 8
blue-footed boobies, 54
blue poison-dart frogs, 10
blue-tongued skinks, 26
bristleworms, 21
bullfrogs, 28–29
bush crickets, 42
butterflies, 14–15

C
cape gannets, 55
cassowaries, 8
caterpillars, 14
cats, 27, 38
cheetahs, 35
chrysalises, 14
cicadas, 28, 42
claws, 55, 56
clown fish, 6–7
Colorado beetles, 10
common yellowthroats, 45
condors, 33
cormorants, 61
crests, 52

crickets, 42–43
crowned cranes, 52
cuttlefish, 19

D
deer, 49
dolphins, 46–47

E
echidnas, 36
eels, 20
eighty-eight butterflies, 15
elephant beetles, 51
elephant seals, 40
elephants, 27, 28–29
emperor moths, 40
eyes, 18, 20

F
fairy wrens, 23
falcons, 32
feathers, 22, 26, 52–53
fiddler crabs, 55
field crickets, 43
fireflies, 16
flamingos, 8–9
flounder, 21
food, gifts of, 40–41, 60
frigate birds, 23
frilled lizards, 27
frogs, 40–41

G
gannets, 33
gardener bowerbirds, 58–59
giant beetles, 50–51
giant pandas, 12
giraffes, 24–25, 35, 48
glass frogs, 20–21
glasswing butterflies, 21
gliding squirrels, 32–33
Goliath beetles, 50
gorillas, 35
grasshoppers, 42, 43
gray wolves, 26
great blue herons, 60
great bowerbirds, 58
green tree pythons, 18–19

H
hairs, 26, 27
hedgehogs, 36, 37
Hercules beetles, 50
hermit crabs, 37
hippopotamuses, 27
hooves, 34, 48
horned owls, 45
horns, 49, 50–51
house wrens, 26
howler monkeys, 29
hummingbirds, 30–31
humpback whales, 46–47

J
jellyfish, 16, 20
Jerusalem crickets, 43
jungle fowl, 48

K
kangaroos, 48–49
katydids, 42
kingfishers, 40–41, 57
kookaburras, 45
krill, 21

L
ladybugs, 11
leaf katydids, 42
leopard toadfish, 47
lions, 28
lizards, 19, 35
lobsters, 36
lyrebirds, 44–45

M
macaroni penguins, 54–55
macaws, 9
magpies, 12
mandrills, 22–23
map butterflies, 15
marsh harriers, 32
moles, 35
monarch butterflies, 11, 14
monkeys, 56
moths, 40
mountain goats, 34
mountain gorillas, 35
mountain sheep, 49

N
naked sea butterflies, 21
nests, 30, 58–61
North American freshwater
    turtles, 56
northern cardinals, 23
nursery web spiders, 60

O
orb-weaving spiders, 41
ostriches, 27

P
painted grasshoppers, 43
panther chameleons, 18
peacocks, 22, 38–39
penguins, 12, 54–55
pied kingfishers, 13
pipevine swallowtail
    caterpillars, 13
poison-arrow frogs, 10
porcupines, 37
porcupine fish, 37
Portuguese man-of-wars, 20
praying mantises, 61
puffins, 22
Raggiana birds of paradise, 53

R
rattail fish, 17
rattlesnakes, 28, 49
regent bowerbirds, 58
robins, 45
rufous hummingbirds, 31

S
satin bowerbirds, 59
sea horses, 55
sea pens, 17
sea urchins, 37
shells, 36–37
Siamese fighting fish, 41
Siberian tigers, 49
signals, 16–17, 46–47
snowy owls, 13
snub-nosed monkeys, 9
songbirds, 44
sounds, 28–29, 31, 41, 42–43
South American butterflies, 15
spiders, 60

spikes, 36–37
spines, 37
squid, 20
stags, 28
stag beetles, 51
starlings, 33
steel blue killifish, 8
stickleback fish, 54
sulfur-crested cockatoos, 52
swallowtail butterflies, 14–15
swallowtail caterpillars, 9
swans, 12

T
tails, 22, 26, 35, 38–39, 44–45,
    46–47, 53, 54
tentacles, 15, 20
thorny devils, 36–37
three-spined stickleback fish, 22
tongues, 14, 26, 35
toxins, 10, 13
tree squirrels, 56
tropical fish, 8
tropical rainforests, 8, 10
trunks, 27
tube anemones, 16
tusks, 27

V
viceroy butterflies, 11
Victoria crowned pigeons, 52
vine snakes, 11
Vogelcap gardener bowerbirds,
    58–59

W
weaver birds, 61
webs, 41
western grebes, 54
whales, 46–47
willow ptarmigans, 18, 45
wings, 14–15, 21, 27, 30–31, 32, 43
wood ducks, 22

Z
zebras, 13, 48

The publisher thanks Puddingburn Publishing Services for the index.

Credits

Key tl=top left; t=top; tc=top center; tr=top right; cl=center left; c=center; cr=center right; bl=bottom left; bc=bottom center; br=bottom right; bg = background

AP = Animal Planet; CBCD = Kodak Photo Disc; CBT = Corbis; iS = istockphoto.com; NGS = National Geographic Society; NHPA = Photoshot; PECD = PhotoEssentials;

SPL = Science Photolibrary; SS = Science and Society Picture Library; SH = Shutterstock; TPL = photolibrary.com

PHOTOGRAPHS
Front cover br, c iS;
1bc AP; **2**bl iS; **3**c iS; **4**tl iS; **5**br AP; **6-7**c iS; **8**tl iS; **9**tr AP; bc CBT; bg, cr iS; **10**bl, br, cr, tc, tr iS; **12**bg, br, tr iS; bl SH; **13**bc AP; bg, tl, tr iS; **14**bc iS; **16**br iS; tr TPL; **17**br CBT; **18**br iS;

19cr iS; **20**bl iS; tr NHPA; **21**br iS; **22**cl iS; **22-23**c AP; bc iS; **23**br, tc, tl, tr iS; **24-25**c AP; **26**tr iS; bl SS; **27**bc, tl iS; **28**bl, c, tl iS; **28-29**c AP; **30**bl, br, tc iS; **31**bc iS, bl iS; br NHPA; **36**tr iS; **36-37**bg iS; **37**bc, cr, tc, tr iS; **38-39**c iS; **40**bc, tl iS; **40-41**bg, tc iS; **41**tr iS; **42**br iS; bl SH; **44-45**bg iS; **45**bl, c, cr, tr iS; tc SH; **46**br iS; **46-47**bg PECD; **47**br TPL; **48**bl, cr iS; **49**br iS; **50**tl iS; tr SPL; **51**tl, tr TPL;

52bl, cl iS; **53**tr iS; **54**tr iS; **54-55** c iS; **55**tr iS; **56**c CBCD; bl iS; **57**tr iS; **58**bl, br TPL; **60**tr TPL; **60-61**bg iS; **62**tl iS; **63**tr iS; br SH

ILLUSTRATIONS
Peter Bull Art Studio 16-17, 29t, 32c, 32t, 52br, 54; Leonello Calvetti 21t, 26c, 32 bl; Dan Cole/The Art Agency 58-59; Barry Croucher/The Art Agency 34-35; Christer Eriksson 40bl, 48-49, 50-51, 53;

John Francis 36-37; Ray Grinaway 42-43t; Gary Hanna/The Art Agency 11; Ian Jackson/The Art Agency 37tl; 46-47, 47cr; David Kirshner 8b, 33; Frank Knight 18-19t; Rob Mancini 61; MBA Studios 45br, 60; Yvan Meunier/Contact Jupiter 9t, 18b, 45c; Terry Pastor/The Art Agency 19b; Mick Posen/The Art Agency 56c, 57; Chris Shields/Wildlife Art 42-43; Guy Troughton 31tc, 44